20p

A first guide to
TREES

SIMON PERRY

Illustrated by
Cecilia Fitzsimons

HODDER AND STOUGHTON
LONDON SYDNEY AUCKLAND TORONTO

To Myfanwy, with thanks

Cé/5582

C6 041193 99

British Library Cataloguing in Publication Data

Perry, Simon
    A first guide to trees.
    1. Trees
    I. Title   II. Fitzsimons, Cecilia
    ISBN 0-340-53108-8

Text copyright © Simon Perry 1991
Artwork copyright © Cecilia Fitzsimons 1991

First published 1991

The author's and publishers' thanks are due to
the following for permission to reproduce photographs:
(t) = top
(b) = bottom
A-Z Collection 10(b), 22(t), 26(t); Heather Angel 12(b),
14(t), 20(b); Aquila Photographics Ltd/Abraham
Cardwell 8(b), 22(b), 24(b); Aquila/E. A. Janes cover,
8(t); Ardea London 14(b); Sdeuard C. Bisserôt 18(t),
18(b); Ron & Christine Foord 16(t); Natural Science
Photos/E. Herbert 12(t); Maurice Nimmo 1, 10(t), 20(t),
24(t), 26(b); Photos Horticultural/Michael Warren 7;
Planet Earth Pictures/Hans Christian Heap 16 (b).

Published by Hodder and Stoughton Children's Books,
a division of Hodder and Stoughton Ltd,
Mill Road, Dunton Green, Sevenoaks, Kent TN13 2YA

Design by Katrina ffiske

Printed in Belgium by Proost International Book
Production

Contents

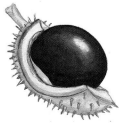

Note to Parents and Teachers

This book introduces children to ten species of tree commonly found throughout the British Isles. The introduction describes general features which will help children identify a type of tree, while the following pages pinpoint individual characteristics which will enable them to identify a specific tree in any season, and to recognise its importance to wildlife and the surrounding landscape.

The place where a tree grows is called its home or habitat. Each kind of tree likes a particular type of habitat. For example, the crack willow generally prefers to live close to water. To help children find the ten trees included in this book, each tree has been given one or more symbols which describe its normal habitats. These are —

woodland: *small woods or large forests*

churchyards

hedgerows

roadside

town parks and school grounds

waterside: *ponds, streams and rivers*

 gardens

However, all ten trees may sometimes be found in other places, especially if they have been planted by people.

In the course of their investigations, children are likely to encounter other, similiar species – for example, the turkey oak, white willow and Corsican pine. This book should enable them to place such trees in their correct group. So, for example, these three trees could clearly be identified as belonging to the 'oak', 'willow' or 'pine' group.

However, there are many other species of tree growing in the British Isles, such as lime and poplar, which have not been included. Also excluded are the many North American, European and Asian trees which have been planted in towns and cities for their attractively coloured leaves. If children wish to find out more about these, other guides will need to be consulted.

Young children are naturally inquisitive about the natural world around them and learn best by active participation. This book is not a substitute for exploration, but a starting point. Encourage children to try the activities on pages 28 to 31, and to use the book as a reference for field identification.

Trees need friends. With this book encourage your children to develop a love of trees and a concern for their care and conservation.

Introduction

Above ground

Trees are very large plants with woody stems called trunks. They have smaller stems called branches which end in twigs. Leaves and flowers grow from the twigs. Leaves have a variety of shapes. In summer, a leaf's shape can help you to name the tree it comes from.

Leaves absorb sunlight to make food for the tree. In autumn and winter there is much less sunshine, so little food can be made. Many trees with soft flat leaves lose their leaves at this time. These trees are called deciduous trees. They rest until the spring when new leaves grow.

Trees which do not lose all their leaves at the same time are called evergreen trees. Many evergreens have tough, shiny needles instead of flat leaves. They often have cones, and for this reason are also known as conifers. There are two evergreens in this book – the Scots pine (p.14) and the yew (p.18).

Look closely at the bark on the trunk of a tree. Can you see anything growing in it? Plants called lichens and mosses can often be found. If a tree or branch is dead and rotting, it may have fungi growing on it.

Below ground

There is more of each tree growing underground. Each tree has a main, woody root which grows straight down and helps to hold the tree firmly. Side roots spread out through the soil. The tips of the finest roots keep growing. They take in the minerals and water needed by the tree. An oak tree has roots which spread as far underground as the branches spread above.

Leaves and flowers

Inside a leaf there are tubes called veins. Water and food pass along the veins to and from the leaf stalk. The stalk joins the leaf to the twig. It can bend so that it does not break in the wind.

Trees have flowers, although these are sometimes difficult to see. The tree below has only one kind of flower. Its sweet smell and colourful petals attract insects which feed on the sugary nectar inside the flower. The insects carry pollen to other flowers. The pollen allows receiving flowers to make seeds, inside a fruit.

hawthorn

Other trees, like the alder, have two types of flower. The first, the male flower, produces pollen. The second, the female, grows into a fruit with seeds. Sometimes, male flowers are long and hanging. They are then called catkins. The wind blows pollen from the catkins to the female flowers.

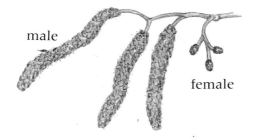

male

female

Spreading the seeds

When seeds have grown inside a fruit, they are ready to leave the tree. Each seed can grow into another tree if it reaches the soil, and if other trees are not growing there. Some seeds are nice to eat and animals carry them away, but a few seeds are dropped. Other seeds are blown away in the wind. Some seeds are inside fruits with wings. These fruits spin like helicopters in the wind and drift away from the tree.

Reaching to the sky

All trees grow upwards towards the sun. Some trees grow taller than others. The tallest trees are often the oldest. This drawing shows the ten trees in this book growing in winter. Each tree is as big as it will grow. Remember that you may find young trees which are smaller.

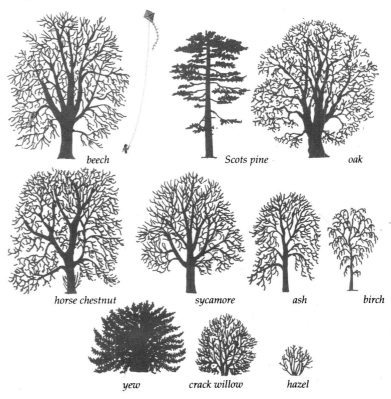

beech

Scots pine

oak

horse chestnut

sycamore

ash

birch

yew

crack willow

hazel

6

How old is a tree?

If you find a tree stump or log on the ground, look at it carefully. The centre is made up of older wood. This is called heartwood. The younger sapwood is around it. The woods may be different colours. Look at the rings in the wood. Each ring shows one year of growth, so if you count the rings, you can find out the age of the stump.

Trees in a wood

Many trees grow close together in a wood. A large wood is called a forest. Some trees and bushes in a wood — for example the birch and hazel — do not grow very tall. They grow under big trees such as oaks.

Some trees, like the hazel, can be cut down to the ground without being killed. The wood can be used to make long poles. The hazel then grows lots more branches. Cutting like this is called coppicing.

Branches may also be cut higher up the trunk. You can often see branches cut in this way on trees by a river or in a street. Cutting like this is called pollarding. The crack willow is often pollarded.

The importance of trees

Trees are important. Trees grow all over the world and are home to many types of animals. They also make a gas called oxygen, which people and animals need to breathe. The wood from trees can be used to make many things, including paper. A line of trees can protect houses and farm crops from wind, and their roots help to stop the soil blowing away.

Trees are also very beautiful. Use this book to find out more about them. Why not try some of the activities suggested at the back of the book?

Oak

A long time ago much of the British Isles was covered with oak trees. The hard wood was used to make ships and furniture. Today large oak trees can still be found in hedgerows, parks and in woods.

The oak grows slowly and can live to a great age. A big tree may be 400 years old. Where a tree is growing in the open, look for twisted branches coming from a short, stout trunk.

▲ Feel the trunk. Oak bark is rough and has many small cracks.

▲ Fresh green leaves appear from the end of April. From the end of May look out for long hanging catkins.

8

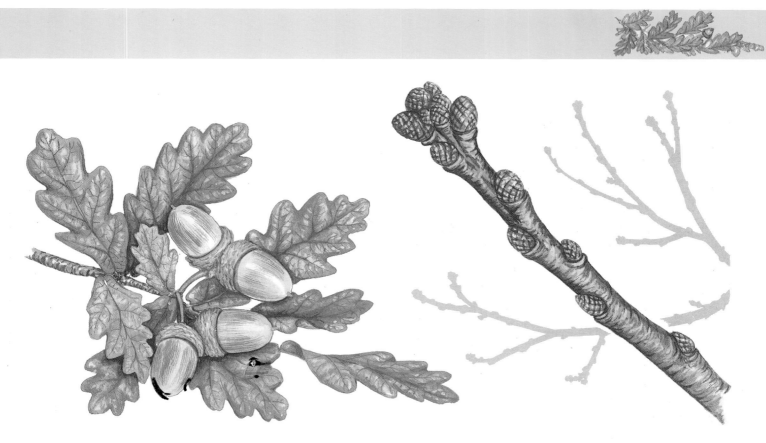

▲ An oak leaf has a very wavy edge. It looks as if bits have been cut out of it. In the autumn you can often find small nuts called acorns, which have fallen to the ground. When on the tree, each acorn sits in a little 'cup'.

▲ In winter look for small brown buds forming a spiral around the twig. At the end of each twig is a little group of buds.

Animals

Many caterpillars like to eat oak leaves. If you shake a branch, you may see them hang down on silken threads. Pigeons and rooks like to eat the acorns. Grey squirrels carry them away to store. The larva of the stag beetle feeds inside rotting oak logs on the ground.

Did you know?

Oak trees are home for more insects than any other British tree. Although many of the insects eat the leaves, the oak can grow more in the summer to replace those it has lost.

9

Beech

Like oaks, beech trees often grow in large woods. A beech wood is often very dark because the thick leaf cover cuts out the sunlight. Any wild flowers living there have to grow early in the year when there are no leaves on the trees.

A beech tree has a tall, straight trunk and large spreading branches. Its roots do not grow deeply into the soil. You can often see the roots spreading from the trunk in all directions.

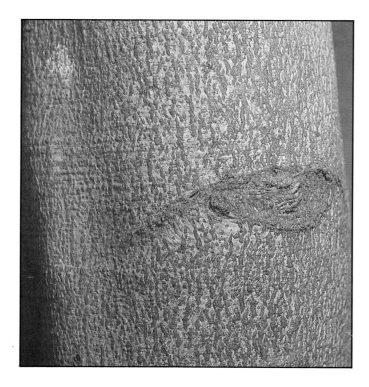

▲ Feel the smooth grey trunk.

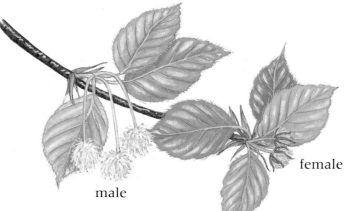

female

male

▲ Look for flowers when the new leaves appear in May. Some of the yellow flowers are on long stalks. The young leaves are shiny green with fine white hairs.

▲ The beech leaf is oval and has a wavy edge. In the autumn the glossy leaves turn to yellow, then reddish-brown as they fall off the tree. At this time there are often large numbers of beech nuts on the ground. These nuts are called beech mast. On the trees the nuts grow in pairs, each pair inside a rough 'coat'.

▲ The brown buds are long and pointed. They zigzag along the twig, which is often hairy.

Animals

Deer, badgers and woodmice like to eat beech mast. Jays will also search for fallen nuts. Grey squirrels damage young beech trees when they eat the bark.

Did you know?

In the last century, people known as bodgers lived in beech woods and made chairs and other pieces of furniture.

Ash

Ash trees often grow in woods, although they are also found in hedgerows.

An ash tree can become very tall. Its branches are spread well apart. The lower branches often curve downwards, while the tips may bend upwards.

▲ Feel the pale, grey bark. On young trees the bark is smooth; on older trees it is ridged.

▲ In spring, small purple flowers come out before the leaves.

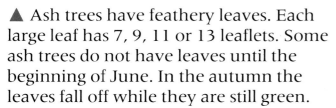

▲ Ash trees have feathery leaves. Each large leaf has 7, 9, 11 or 13 leaflets. Some ash trees do not have leaves until the beginning of June. In the autumn the leaves fall off while they are still green.

Ash seeds are attached to a long wing to carry them in the wind. They are called ash keys and hang from the tree in clusters.

▲ In winter look for grey twigs with black buds.

Animals

Rooks often make their large twiggy nests where a number of ash trees grow together. A group of nests like this is called a rookery.

Although ash seeds are very small, sometimes there are large numbers of them. They are an important source of food for bank voles and wood mice. In ash woods, if it is a bad year for seeds, there will be fewer of these small mammals.

Did you know?

There is an old saying about oak and ash leaves, and which come out first.

Ash out before oak, in for a soak.
It will be a wet summer.
Oak out before ash, in for a splash.
It will be a fairly dry summer.

Is this saying true? Why not find out for yourself.

Ash fruits are called keys because each seed and wing has the outline of an old-fashioned key used for opening doors or chests.

13

Scots Pine

Many types of pine are found in the British Isles, but only the Scots pine grows here naturally. This beautiful tree is an evergreen. It is found in Scottish forests, but has been planted in many other places with sandy soil.

Young trees have the shape of a Christmas tree. Older trees lose some of their lower branches so that gaps appear between the branches still left.

▲ Feel the trunk. Near the ground the bark is grey and rough. Higher up the bark may have peeled. Here the trunk and branches look red.

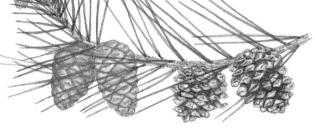

▲ In the summer you may see how the flowers develop into the cones which carry the seeds. The tiny, red female flowers may be seen from the end of April. Further back the green cones grow in pairs. The cones turn brown after two years and fall from the tree.

▲ The leaves of pine trees are called needles. The Scots pine has needles in pairs. They are blue-green in colour and slightly twisted.

▲ As the cones open up in dry weather, the winged seeds fall out.

Animals

Red squirrels like to live in pine trees over twenty-five years old. One squirrel may gnaw through more than 20,000 cones in a year! Look out for the common coal tit and tiny goldcrest which feed on the seeds. Rare birds of prey, such as the sparrow-hawk and osprey, often use tall Scots pine trees to nest in.

Did you know?

The tallest trees in the world are redwood trees. These are conifers similar to the Scots pine. The oldest tree is a pine called the bristlecone. Some bristlecone pines have been alive for over 4000 years.

Pine cones can be used to tell the weather. They open up in dry warm weather and close when the air is wet.

Silver Birch

There are two kinds of birch tree with a silvery trunk. They grow on different soils, so silver birch trees can be found anywhere in the British Isles. Look for them in woods, hedges, parks and gardens.

Each type of birch has a different shape. This warty birch has long drooping branches. You may also find the hairy birch, which has upright twisting branches.

▲ Feel the bark. It is often very rough and black at the bottom. Higher up it is silvery-white. It often has black diamond shapes.

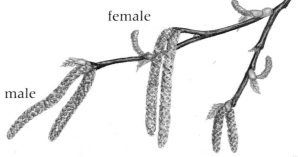

female

male

▲ Birch flowers open in April just before the leaves. The male catkins, which produce pollen, look like lambs' tails. The female catkins look like green caterpillars.

16

▲ The shiny, triangle-shaped leaves have ragged edges. In autumn they turn yellow before falling. The catkins are now full of tiny winged seeds which may be carried a long way by the wind.

▲ Birch twigs are thin and whip-like. They have very small green and brown buds. The warty birch has little rough warts on a smooth twig.

Animals

Small birch trees are often left to grow in pine woods. Deer and hares like to feed on the young shoots. Old dying birch trees often have holes made by woodpeckers for their nests. When the woodpeckers have left, the holes may be used by bats.

Did you know?

Birch trees can grow higher up mountains than any other deciduous tree. They quickly appear wherever there is bare ground, without being planted. Some birches have a disease which cause bundles of tiny twigs to grow very close together. The bundles look like large birds' nests and are known as witches' brooms.

17

Yew

Yew trees can be found in woods. Look for them also in churchyards and parks.

The evergreen yew tree has a thick cover of branches and leaves and a short trunk. Sometimes there appear to be several large branches near the ground. They are in fact new trunks growing around an old tree.

▲ The bark on a yew tree trunk is light brown. It flakes off to leave reddish patches.

female

male

▲ The male and female flowers usually grow on different trees. They are very small and blossom underneath the leaves.

▲ Yew leaves are flat, pointed needles. They are glossy on top and pale green underneath.

▲ The cones of the yew tree look like red berries. Inside, are the hard brown seeds. Look for them in late summer.

Animals

The red juicy flesh of the berries is eaten by many animals, including badgers and thrushes. The poisonous seeds pass through their bodies without harming them. **But do not eat the berries yourself.**

Did you know?

Yew trees can become very old. Some people believe they can grow for 1000 years, making them the oldest living things in Britain. In large parks and gardens, yew trees are often trimmed into the shapes of animals. Yew trees may first have been planted in churchyards in order to shelter people meeting while the church was being built.

Hazel

At one time large coppices (or copses) of hazel were grown to make into small poles. Hazel trees can still be found in many woods, although they may not be cut back any more. They are also often found growing in hedgerows.

Hazel usually grows as a bush or small tree with a thick cover of leaves. If it has been cut back, it has many branches.

female

male

▲ Feel the smooth shiny bark of a young coppiced hazel. It is greenish-brown. The trunk of an older tree is more rugged and scaly.

▲ The male catkins hang like lambs' tails. They may be seen throughout the winter. The little red tassels of the female flowers can be seen in February or March.

▲ The broad hazel leaf is rough and hairy. It has a pointed tip.

▲ The nut is wrapped in a leafy cup. By autumn it is brown and hard and ready to eat.

Animals

Hazel nuts (or cob nuts) are eaten by many animals. Squirrels, jays, and pigeons balance on bending branches to reach unripe nuts. Bank voles and wood mice eat ripe nuts which have fallen to the ground.

Did you know?

In the past hazel poles were used as wattles in building. The wattles were woven together to form a house frame, and then mud and straw, called daub, were plastered on top.

The rare dormouse is found only where there are plenty of hazel trees. In some countries it is known as the hazel mouse. Dormice get fat on hazel nuts and black-berries before sleeping for seven months through the winter.

Crack Willow

The crack willow grows beside rivers and streams and in damp woods. In the past it was pollarded every four or five years, producing lots of long, straight poles.

The crack willow can grow to become a large tree if it is never pollarded. However, if a pollarded tree is not regularly cut, the branches can break off and the trunk crack under the weight. Red rootlets can often be seen in the water.

▲ Feel the deeply ridged, grey bark. **Do not go too close to the water's edge.** Touch the tree on the side farthest away from the water.

male

female

▲ The flowers, known as catkins, usually open after the leaves. But the catkins of the sallow, or pussy willow, come out before the leaves. On some crack willows you may see green female catkins. The yellow male catkins grow on other crack willows.

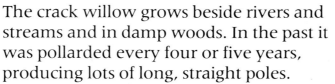

▲ The leaves are long, thin and pointed. They are shiny green on top and grey-green underneath. Look out for white, woolly seeds blowing off the catkins.

▲ The buds are light brown and hairy. They curve into a point.

Animals

Otters may live in holes called holts among the roots of old willow trees, but they are now quite rare. Little owls sometimes nest in pollarded crack willow trees.

Did you know?

The tree is called crack, or brittle willow because its twigs easily snap off. They are then washed away in the water. If the twigs become lodged in the river bank, they produce roots and can grow into new trees. The long roots of the crack willow hold the soil and stop the bank being washed away.

Another type of willow tree is grown especially for making cricket bats. Other types are used for making baskets.

23

Sycamore

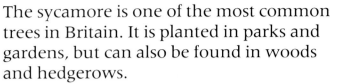

The sycamore is one of the most common trees in Britain. It is planted in parks and gardens, but can also be found in woods and hedgerows.

The sycamore grows quickly to become a large tree. It has thick branches and a dense cover of leaves.

▲ Feel the rough, flaky bark of a large sycamore tree. At first the bark is smooth but then it peels off. It is light brown underneath.

▲ The flowers hang in long bunches. They open out with the leaves in May.

24

▲ Sycamore leaves have five 'fingers' (or lobes) joined together. The stalks are often red. In autumn look for the fat, winged seeds spinning down to the ground.

▲ The rough twigs of sycamores have big green buds which grow opposite each other along the twig.

Animals

Sycamore flowers produce a lot of nectar, which attract bees in spring. Grey squirrels like to eat the young bark and may kill some branches as a result. Very few animals need to eat sycamore leaves, but a large tree can provide useful shelter for birds.

Did you know?

Sycamore trees grow well everywhere in Britain. They are often planted to form a shelter for farms and houses high up on hills. Gardeners sometimes dislike sycamores because in the spring the ground can be covered by tiny seedlings. However, large sycamores can be very beautiful, especially in the autumn when the leaves change colour.

The horse chestnut is also known as the conker tree. It is often grown in parks and along roads.

This beautiful big tree has a dense cover of large leaves. Older trees may have lower branches which curve upwards.

▲ Feel the rough bark. It is greyish-brown in colour. Older trees often have knobbly trunks.

▲ In May look out for large flowers at the tips of the branches. Horse chestnut trees are often planted because of their beautiful white or pink candle-like flowers.

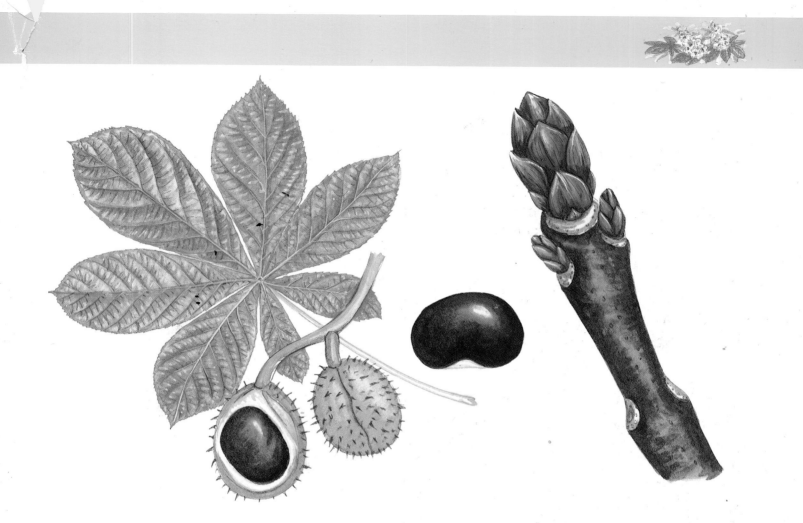

▲ Horse chestnut leaves have five or seven separate 'fingers' (or lobes). They look like large hands. In autumn the conkers ripen inside green spiny cases.

▲ The large twigs of the horse chestnut have sticky brown buds. Look also for the horseshoe-shaped scars where the leaves have fallen.

Animals

The candle-like flowers provide nectar for bees and other insects. In large country parks conkers are eaten by cattle and deer. Unlike sweet chestnuts, horse chestnuts cannot be eaten by people.

Did you know?

The name conker comes from conqueror, which means winner. Before horse chestnut trees grew in Britain, the game of conkers was played with hazel nuts or snail shells.

Activities

Winter

In winter, when many trees do not have leaves, there are still lots of things you can do. First choose a tree, growing on its own. Find out how thick its trunk is. Try hugging it. Do your fingers touch? If not, use a piece of string to measure it.

Next find out how tall it is. All you need is a pencil and a tape measure. Stand several metres away from the tree and hold out your pencil so that it appears to be the same size as the tree. Keeping the bottom of the pencil level with the bottom of the tree, lay your pencil flat, just as if you had cut down the tree. Look where the top of the pencil now appears to be. Walk to this spot, or ask a friend to do so. Now measure the distance from this spot to the tree and you will discover how tall the tree is.

Winter is also a good time to make bark rubbings. You will need some plain paper and wax crayons. Hold some paper firmly against a tree trunk and scribble over it gently with a wax crayon. Do this with other trees to see how your rubbings differ.

Spring

In spring, you can make leaf rubbings. Place a leaf upside down on a table and put some paper on top. Hold the paper steady and rub with a wax crayon.

You can also make a cast of a leaf by pressing it into a flat piece of plasticine. Take away the leaf, and look at the network of leaf veins left in the plasticine.

Later in spring or summer, your tree will be covered with leaves. Try looking at them with a small mirror or mirror tile on the ground. Can you see how each leaf is joined to a twig, how the twigs are joined to branches, and how the branches are joined to the trunk?

Place a piece of paper on a board or book next to the mirror. Kneel down and look into the mirror. Can you draw some of those leaves and twigs?

Summer

By the end of summer, some of the leaves you have looked at will have been eaten by insects. Find an oak tree. Look on the undersides of the leaves for tiny orange spots. These are called spangle galls. They are made by tiny wasps which lay their eggs inside the leaves. There are other types of galls on twigs and acorns.

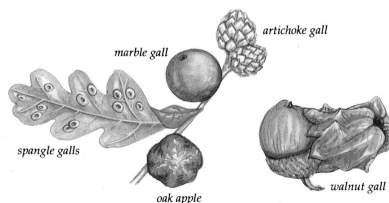

marble gall

artichoke gall

spangle galls

oak apple

walnut gall

Autumn

In autumn, nuts and seeds are easy to find. Many, like beech mast and hazelnuts, are carried away by animals. Can you find the remains of any which have been eaten by animals? Some nuts may have holes nibbled by mice or voles; pine cones may be stripped of their seeds by squirrels. Find acorns with tiny holes through which beetles have eaten their way out.

squirrel

mouse or vole

weevil

squirrel

Autumn is the time that many trees lose their leaves. They fall to the ground and begin to rot into the soil. Can you find leaves of different colours? Hold them up to the sky to see the colours and patterns of veins. Make a collection of leaves from one type of tree. Start with the green leaves, then look for yellow and brown leaves, and finally rotting leaf skeletons.

Food chain mobile

Many animals live together in a wood. They depend on each other for their food. They are linked together in a 'food chain'. In an oak wood, for example, leaves on the trees are eaten by caterpillars, while the dead leaves on the ground are eaten by snails. Blue tits eat some of the caterpillars and thrushes eat some of the snails. Sparrowhawks eat both the blue tits and thrushes.

You can make a food chain mobile like the one shown here. Trace the outline of each of the pictures on to some card. Colour in the pictures and thread them together.

Grow your own trees

Collect seeds in autumn and start a tree nursery in your garden or school grounds. Collect seeds like acorns and ash keys before it gets too cold or they will be eaten. Look for healthy fat seeds. Store them in a dry place or plant them straightaway.

What you do:

1 Place small stones in a plant pot so that water can drain through.

2 Fill three-quarters of the pot with soil. Water the soil but don't make it too wet.

3 Put one seed (e.g. an acorn) in the pot.

4 Cover the seed with more soil. Put the pot in a cool place for the winter.

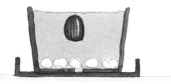

5 In spring, you could put the pot inside a cut-off plastic bottle. This acts as a mini greenhouse, and also keeps the soil moist.

6 In autumn, or the following spring, dig a small hole and carefully plant the seedling tree. Remember to keep it watered. You may need to use wire netting to protect your tree from squirrels and rabbits.

If you have enjoyed reading this book, why not join WATCH, the national wildlife and environment club for children? Each year WATCH organises exciting projects on wildlife and conservation for all the family through a network of WATCH groups. In your area these are run by your local Wildlife Trust. For a membership leaflet and more information write to:

WATCH
The Royal Society of Nature
Conservation (RSNC)
Witham Park
Waterside South
Lincoln LN5 7JN

Index

This index does not include the names of the ten trees covered by this book. Each of these is listed on the Contents page.